Investing Basics

presents:

Stock Investing Successfully For Beginners

(w/ FREE BONUSES)

Making Money with Stocks in just a FEW HOURS!

F.R. Commerce

3rd Edition

Special thanks to:

The Investing Basics Team

The Stock Market Investing Association

Stock Trading Group

The Investing Club

Business and Investors Association

and many more people who have helped contribute to this work

Table of Contents

Disclaimer:

While all attempts have been made to verify the information provided in this book, the author does not assume any responsibility for errors, omissions, or contrary interpretations of the subject matter contained within. **The information provided in this book is for educational and entertainment purposes only. The reader is responsible for his or her own actions and the author does not accept any responsibilities for any liabilities or damages, real or perceived, resulting from the use of this information.**

Introduction

The realm of the affluent are well too familiar with the world of stocks. They know where and how to invest their amassed fortunes, only to grow those fortunes even further as their investments grow in value. Also, those same investments continue to pay off the owners somehow - through dividends, interest, gains, and so on.

But here's the best news. That skill - successfully investing in stocks - is not limited to just the affluent. Fortunately, you don't need to have a business degree to earn profits in stocks either.

But first...

Are you willing to learn further?

Are you not afraid to fail?

Do you have the will and focus to move forward? No matter how bad the news and markets blare at you?

If you answered yes to all the above, carry on. (if not, you may wanna return this book. Stocks are NOT for the weak!)

Good. now let's move forward.

The following first few chapters introduce you to the world of stocks. They will give you some background in stocks, so you'll be able to understand how this investment product works and how it can help you build your wealth.

In the next chapters, by practicing some simple guidelines such as making regular investments in proven companies, risks can be minimized. Adequate knowledge can help you make sound decisions. Hence, the most basic rule in investing is: Know what you're getting into!

Besides learning the ropes on all the most basic concepts and tools to enable you to understand the stock market, you'll also find everything you need to find your feet in the realms of research. You will learn where to look for the tell-tale signs of a great company, and exactly what to look for.

Finally, you can read about some of the Investment world Giants, like Warren Buffet and others, and share some of their tried and tested techniques for yourself.

Congratulations again for buying my book. Now press on to victory.

PART I: What Stocks Are & How They Work

Chapter 1: Stocks Explained

Investopedia defines stocks as *"a type of security that signifies ownership in a corporation and represents a claim on part of the corporation's assets and earnings."*

This statement clearly says that a stock owner or shareholder is an owner of a company. The ownership depends entirely on the number of shares that a person owns - relative to the number of outstanding shares. Suppose a company has 100 shares of outstanding stocks and one person owns 10 shares. This means that this person owns and has claim to 10% of that company's assets.

Do you want to share in the growth and profits of established businesses such as Coca-Cola, Microsoft, Ford or Facebook? You certainly can! All you have to do is to buy shares of their stock either directly or through brokerage firms. A word of caution, just because these companies will continue to make money in the future, it doesn't automatically guarantee that the value of their stocks will increase. Microsoft's stock value can decrease as well as Ford's or Coca-Cola's or Facebook's over time. But at least every time you avail of their products and services, you'll have some satisfaction knowing that part of what you paid returns to you.

From the established business point-of-view, they have great incentives to issue a stake in their ownership and earnings.

For example, let's say that after spending a considerable amount of time developing your career, you have finally decided to be your own boss. Let's say Baking has always been your passion and at this point you have decided to spend some time developing this skill.

As you become more confident with your baking skills you begin to share some baked goodies as presents or give-aways during special occasions. Eventually, your friends begin to order from you. Seeing that there is a market for your products, you decide to take them to the local bakeshops.

Suppose that a popular coffee shop became interested in dealing with you as their supplier. To meet the demand, you've decided to put in more hours and hire a few more people. It doesn't take long before other retailers notice the quality of your products and decide to offer you contracts.

Profits have started to roll in. At this point, you are earning more than your day job and have decided to quit entirely.

The business is certainly expanding as your client base grows. You need more time to focus on the day to day tasks. In order to keep up, you will also need to source out funds to finance additional equipment, manpower and system upgrades. The bottom line: you will need lots and lots of money.

One way to do that is to go to the financial markets and, with the help of other institutions and agencies such as Investment Bankers, issue your company's stocks. Other individuals can claim some ownership, as well as a possible fraction of the earnings, in exchange for funding your company's growth. And now you see what stocks are and what they're for.

Chapter 2: Further Defining Stocks

In this chapter, we discuss basic concepts about stocks and the stock market to equip individual investors with simple investing concepts.

Gambling?

A common misconception about investing in stocks is that it commonly resembles gambling. If luck is on your side, you can double or triple your money overnight or even in a matter of seconds. Likewise, if you're just unlucky, all your capital and your earnings can be wiped out in a blink of an eye. If the stock market is as haphazard and unpredictable as gambling then why do more companies go public? More importantly, how did Warren Buffet earn millions through stocks?

The stock market is definitely not a casino. It's a far cry from it. Buying shares of stock are a way for people of different income classes to invest in companies to build wealth. In fact, stocks grow in value over time. History shows that stocks are profitable long term investments. The following figure shows the total real returns of several asset classes:

FIGURE 1. TOTAL REAL RETURN INDEXES, 1802 THROUGH DECEMBER 2006

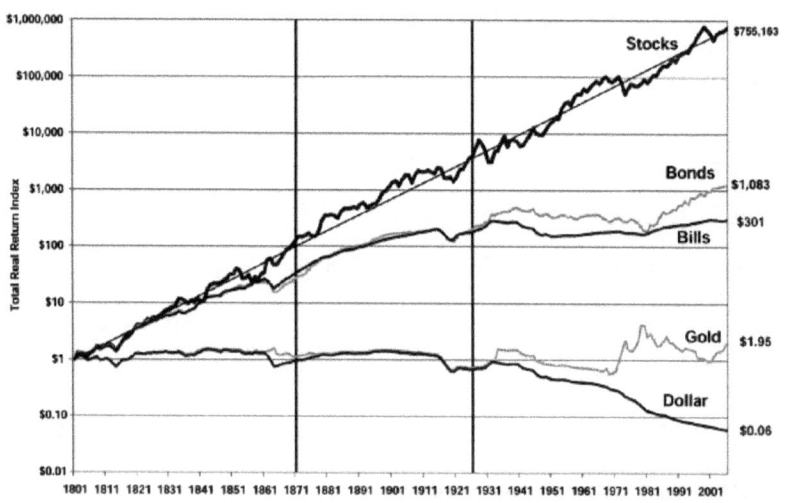

Stocks More In Detail

Remember that a stock is simply defined as a share in ownership of a company. As a proof of ownership, it also allows you to have a claim on a company's profits and assets. As you continue to acquire more shares, your ownership stake increases. The terms equity, share, stock are used interchangeably since they all mean the same.

Each stock is represented by a stock certificate. Prior to the computer age, these documents are issued to each shareholder. These fancy pieces of papers contain the name of the company and the shareholder. In order to make a trade, the shareholder has to physically take the certificates to a brokerage firm.

Currently, stock certificates are stored electronically by your broker. This system eliminates the process of going to the broker's office to complete a trade. The current trading platforms also facilitate easier handling of transactions such that the investor can immediately buy or sell stocks without having to wait in line or repeatedly calling until a broker becomes available to process a transaction.

For those who would want a hardcopy of the certificates, you can request them from your broker for a certain fee. The disadvantage is that this makes you solely responsible for the document. Any damage on the document may nullify your shares or stake in a certain company.

What does it mean to be a shareholder?

Being a part owner of a publicly listed company doesn't imply that you have to be involved in the day-to-day operations of the business. In fact, the extent of your involvement is at most, equivalent to one vote per share to elect a member of the board of directors, usually held at annual meetings.

It is the role of the top management committee to ensure that the value of the company is increasing. In theory, certain shareholders can vote to change the management if this goal is not achieved. In reality, however, only people who own significant numbers of shares (such as institutional investors and big time entrepreneurs), or shares with defined voting rights, are entitled to have a say in important issues. Their opinion can influence how a company is run.

Having a say in how the company is managed should not be a big deal for ordinary investors. It should be the least of their worries. At the end of the day, you, as an ordinary investor, should just want to make your money work for you - not the other way around.

The essence of being a shareholder is the entitlement to a slice of the company's profits and be able to have a claim on its assets. Profits are paid out to investors in the form of dividends. The value of your dividend is proportional to the amount of shares you have. Sometimes dividends are given in the form of cash or in the form of additional stocks.

Are we liable for holding stocks?

In case a company has debts, does being a stock holder make you liable for it? The good news is NO. A stock has limited liability.

This feature exempts you, as a shareholder, from being personally liable in case the company has no capacity to pay its debts. This set-up differs from that of partnerships; wherein partners are held liable. Hence, creditors can go after the corporation's assets as payment for debt. If the company isn't incorporated, each partner or majority shareholder may be asked for their personal assets instead.

In owning a stock, the most you can lose is just equivalent to the overall value of your investment. This means that if the company, of which you are a stock holder, goes bankrupt, you lose your investment and not your personal assets.

Are you worried yet? If not, read on.

BONUS PRACTICE: Company Doing Well?

How are your companies doing?

List five of your favourite public corporate companies (if they have stocks getting traded in stock markets worldwide, they're public companies).

Then,

Check their corporate website and look for their most recent EARNINGS RELEASES. It should be on their investor/financial information section. For example, you can find Apple's most recent earning statements on their main website, apple.com. Then, you can view the support section, and then investor relations. Their earnings releases should be within the Financial Relations section.

Then, ask yourself, "Will this company be doing well or not?" You just need to make an opinion.

See, this is what separates you from the "pretender" stock investors, who just keep reading and looking for "hot tips" and "insights" - without actually doing anything about it. You're actually going to move through and practice the material.

Building a Habit

This is just basic, yet absolutely important research that all experienced investors do. They might do it in different ways, but they NEED to find good information before placing their investment.

PART II: Fundamental Stock Terms to Know

Chapter 3: Stock Terms

What are the different types of stocks?

Various kinds of stocks can be issued by companies. Essentially, there are two types: common stock and preferred stock.

☐ *Common Stock*: When people talk about stock, this is usually the type they are referring to. Common stocks are shares representing ownership of a portion of a company and a claim on profits and assets. Remember the voting right we talked about earlier? Owning common stocks gives you that right.

Common stocks entail the most risk compared to other types, yet it comes with higher returns. One disadvantage is that when a company goes bankrupt, common shareholders cannot receive a single cent until all creditors, bond holders and preferred shareholders have been paid first.

Preferred Stock: Like common stocks, preferred stocks also represent a degree of ownership in the company minus the voting rights. An advantage of having preferred shares is that you are guaranteed a fixed dividend forever as long as you have that stock. Another advantage is that in case the company goes bankrupt, preferred shareholders are paid first before common shareholders.

 Other Classes of Stock: Some companies issue other forms of stock aside from the two types mentioned. The primary reason for this is to retain the voting power of a certain group. It is possible that different classes of stock may have different voting rights. For instance, one class of shares would be held by a certain group that has twenty votes per share, while another class of shares would be issued to majority of the investors that has a right of one vote per share.

The claim to assets is most relevant if and when the company becomes bankrupt. Common shareholders receive a part of what's left, upon liquidation, after all the debts have been paid. Preferred shareholders on the other hand, receive an amount proportional to their share since they have a higher claim.

Again, the importance of being a shareholder (as a simple investor) does not rest on your capacity to influence how a company is run. Leave that to the Board of Directors. Rather, it is your entitlement on the profits and claim on the assets that gives value to your stock certificate - and ultimately growing your investments.

Earning through Stocks

As discussed previously, owning shares of stock represent ownership of a company. This entitles the holder to a claim on a portion of the assets and profits of a company, depending on the amount of shares owned. But how exactly do you earn profit from this ownership? Stock investors earn profit from in two ways:

    ☐   *Price appreciation* – if the price per share of the stock you have increases to a level higher than the price at which you bought it, you gain profits. For example, you bought a stock of company ABC at $5 per share. After some time the price doubles to $10 per share. You now have a total earning of $5 per share. Note that this profit is realized only when you sell the stock at $10 each. Only then will you have *capital gain*. Likewise, it is also possible to lose profit if the share price decreases to a level lower than your buying price.

☐ *Dividends* – Companies generate profits annually. In some cases most or all of these are reinvested into the business. Often times, several companies give back this wealth to shareholders either in the form of cash or additional shares.

Summing dividends and the effect of price appreciation will give you an idea of your overall return. It is important to note that the performance of each stock and the amount of dividends vary for each listed company.

Chapter 4: Defining The Stock Market

As you flip through the business section of the newspaper, you might have come across the following headlines:

- European markets to fall on Ukraine fears

- Stocks slip on pre-weekend caution;

- Major indexes post weekly gains

- S & P 500 is up 1.3% for the week to date

The stock market exists in several parts of the world. Different countries have their trading platforms - which may vary in size. Developed countries may have more established markets composed of a larger number of companies of different capacities. Emerging countries on the other hand may have a young stock exchange platform composed of fewer but well established companies. In any case, the function of an exchange remains the same in any part of the globe.

Investing in stocks is usually done within the stock market. Just like a typical market where there are tons of items to trade with money, the stock market is a venue for buying and selling shares of several listed companies. It exists to facilitate the exchange of shares between buyers and sellers.

The full definition, in simple and common terms, is "a market wherein shares of publicly listed companies are issued and traded through exchanges or over-the-counter markets."

It is also known as the equity market, wherein companies are provided access to capital in exchange for giving investors a piece of ownership in the company. It gives small investors an opportunity to grow their capital - without the risks entailed in running a business or the sacrifices that accompany a lucrative career.

Of course, as a part owner, investors become part of the financial milestones or setbacks of a company whose shares they hold. If the company is profitable, investors earn through dividends and price appreciation. Consequently, if a company loses money, the stock price may go down and the investors lose if they sell the stock at the lower prevailing price.

Market Types Explained

Perhaps you have heard about primary markets and secondary markets and you might have wondered what its relevance to the stock market is. You may have even asked yourself how many stock market types are there...

Primary Markets

On the one hand, securities are created (via IPO – Initial Public Offering) in primary markets. It is basically a market in which companies sell stocks to the public for the first time.

When a company decides to go public, a set of requirements has to be fulfilled first.

One, an underwriting firm should be contacted to identify the legal and financial details of a public offering.

Two, filing of a preliminary registration statement, known as the preliminary prospectus, should be made with the appointed authorities. The statement should detail the company's prospects and interests. Note that this document is neither a solicitation nor is it finalized. It is simply a set of documents that describes the company's intent.

Three, the appointed authorities must approve the finalized statement and the final prospectus, the document that details the stock price, benefits, restrictions. It is a legally binding document for the company and its would-be shareholders. In primary markets, the stocks are purchased straight from the issuing company.

Secondary Markets

When people talk about the stock market, they usually refer to the secondary market. It is formally defined as the venue where investors can trade previously issued securities minus the involvement of the issuing companies.

In the secondary market, investors buy shares from other investors. This is what we commonly recognize as the "stock market". It encompasses the New York Stock Exchange, Nasdaq, and all the other exchanges around the globe. In this case, the issuing company is not involved in any way in the exchange. Investors trade with fellow investors who own the shares that you would like to either buy or sell.

Secondary markets are further subdivided into auction markets and dealer markets:

Auction Market

A feature of an auction market is that all parties interested to trade securities, either as an individual or institution, assemble in an area and announce their target buying or selling price - or the bid and ask price. The aim of this system is to bring all parties together until each has found a counterpart offering an agreeable deal.

Dealer Market

In the case of a dealer market, all parties do not have to assemble in a central hub. Market participants are connected via electronic networks. In this system, the dealers have an inventory of securities which they can buy or sell to the market participants. Different dealers offer a spread of prices where they would like to buy or sell the securities. This option gives investors an idea of the best possible price that they can avail in making a trade.

BONUS PRACTICE: Viewing the Stock Markets

Each developed nation should have a stock market exchange.

What you're going to do is go to the following stock markets, depending on where you are located:

- United States: NYSE, nyse.com

- EU Countries: Euronext, euronext.com

- United Kingdom: London Stock Exchange, londonstockexchange.com

- Canada: Toronto Stock Exchange, tmx.com

If your country isn't included above (or your country isn't part of the EU), simply search online for your country's stock exchange market.

Then, list the exchange's top five best-performing stocks. This will give you an idea of what companies are on the rise, as well as what industries are growing and doing well.

If you like, you can also do some deeper research. For one of the companies you find, look for their competitors, as well as their partner companies. This give you an idea how well an industry is doing.

Chapter 5: The Stock Market Index

To have a general picture of how a stock market performs, an index of stocks can be consulted. These indices can represent either the whole market or a particular market segment.

Essentially, an index is a measure of the changes in a portfolio of stocks. Since it would be too difficult to track all the stocks traded in the country, it makes more sense to study the prices of a smaller set of stocks that more or less mimics the trend of the stock exchange. This system is similar to the way pollsters utilize political surveys to gauge the public sentiment. In the case of investors, indices are used to assess the performance of the exchange.

The Dow Jones

When someone asks you: How is the market doing? That person usually refers to the US stock market. More specifically, the Dow Jones Industrial Average. This is a widely watched index that tracks the performance of 30 big companies based in the United States. Among these are fast-food giant McDonald's, aircraft manufacturer Boeing, popular beverage maker Coca-Cola, IT pioneers IBM, Microsoft and Intel, pharmaceutical behemoths Pfizer and Merck and oil titan Exxon Mobil.

Other Indices

Although a renowned index, the Dow has received several criticisms due to the relatively small number of companies that may inadequately represent the actual condition of the U.S. stock exchange. The following lists the other market indexes available as well as a simple description of the types of stocks that they track:

⬜ **Standard & Poor's 500**: This stock price index began in 1923 and was called the Standard and Poor's. By 1926, it became the Standard and Poor's composite index which contained 90 stocks. The index was expanded on March 4, 1957 and was then named the S & P 500 index.

Compared to the Dow Jones Industrial Average, the S & P 500 has a hefty portfolio. It tracks the performance of 500 large companies based in the U.S. These companies account for more than 70% of the total market value of the thousands of stocks traded in America. Hence, it is a better representation of the large company stocks in the country compared to Dow. The S & P 500 index is calculated by adding the total market value of its component stocks, not just the current share price.

☐ **Russell 2000**: As the name implies, the market value of 2,000 smaller US company stocks from different industries are tracked by this index. While it may be logical to speculate that small company stocks tend to follow the trend of larger company stocks, it is usual for one index to rise or fall more than the other or to move contrary to the other.

As an example, consider the year 2001 wherein the S & P 500 fell 11.9% even as the Russell 2000 rose 2.5%. The opposite happened in 2007 wherein S & P 500 gained 5.5% while Russell 2000 lost 1.6%. It is important to note that in general, small company stocks tend to be more volatile compared to large company stocks.

☐ **Wilshire 5000**: Unlike Russell 2000, the Wilshire 5000 index doesn't track 5,000 company stocks. It actually tracks a total of 4,000 stocks owned by companies based in the US. The company sizes included in this index range from small, medium to large. Hence, it is considered the broadest index that adequately represents the US stock market.

☐ **Morgan Stanley EAFE**: The acronym EAFE stands for Europe, Australasia, and Far East. That being said, this index tracks the prices of stocks of developed countries in these regions. The performance of this index can give shareholders a glimpse of the economic activity in other developed countries and perhaps compare their performance with that of the US.

Morgan Stanley Emerging Markets: As the name implies, this index tracks the value of stocks in less economically developed but emerging nations. Among these markets are Korea, Mexico, Brazil, China, Russia, Taiwan, India and South Africa. Compared to stocks in developed markets, emerging markets tend to be more volatile.

One advantage though is that it doesn't exactly reflect the patterns of developed markets. Hence, in some cases developed markets may drop while emerging markets continue to gain profits.

 NASDAQ: The acronym stands for National Association of Securities Dealers Automated Quotations which was an automated quotation system that was developed on February 8, 1971. During this period the system revolutionized the method of trading stocks. Prior to its launch, quotations of 'over-the-counter' (OTC) stocks were submitted by principal traders or brokerage houses that have an inventory of these. After that, each type of stock will be assigned to a specialist, who is in charge of maintaining an orderly market on that particular stock.

With NASDAQ, quotes were disseminated quickly since it has a database linked to more than 500 market makers nationwide. It quickly became a niche for small and new firms which have recently gone public or those that did not meet the listing requirements of the larger exchange platforms such as the New York Exchange. What's more, the computerized system became a second home for most of the young tech firms

Eventually, NASDAQ evolved into an industry specific index. It tracks the performance of the top tech firms in the US which includes Microsoft, Apple, Google, Intel and Cisco Systems. While the performance of this is strongly linked to the condition of the tech industry, it may not reflect the overall scenario of the US stock market.

In hindsight, indices are simply lists of stocks. Anybody could create one! But what distinguishes the major indices from the smaller ones is the reputation and credibility of the company who created the index. The Dow Jones & Company, who owns the Dow, is the same group behind The Wall Street Journal.

Why do we look at indices?

Investors look at indices for a number of reasons. The most common is that it can give you an idea how particular stocks perform in comparison to another type of stock.

Consider the year 1998 wherein the S & P 500 was up by 28.6% while Russell 2000 was down by 2.5%. Morgan Stanley EAFE rose 20.3% in that same year. Fast forward to 2001, both the S & P 500 and Morgan Stanley EAFE fell, at 11.9% and 21.4% respectively. With this information, you can manage your portfolio and minimize risks. For example, you may choose to allocate 60% of your portfolio to large company stocks since they are relatively stable while 10% goes to small company stocks since these are more volatile.

Another reason for looking into indices is that it gives you a benchmark from which you can assess the performance of your stock investments. If your portfolio contains mostly large company stocks, a good index to follow is the S & P. Likewise, the Russell 2000 index will give you an idea how small company stocks perform while the Wilshire 5000 index can give you an overview of the price trends in various types of companies.

Choose the appropriate benchmark for your portfolio. Doing so will allow you to assess the performance of your stocks properly. Assuming you own a fund that primarily invests in large US companies. It would certainly be useless comparing your investment to the Nasdaq index or the Russell 2000 index.

Chapter 6:What Drives Price Fluctuations?

You might ask, "why the heck do stock prices change?". No one truly knows the definite answer. A variety of factors combine to affect the trends we are seeing now.

No one can predict the future. The end of the world is prophesied to occur in the 21st century - yet we are still here, at this point, eagerly learning the ropes to stock investing...

While there may be tons of literature and studies proposing the future market trends, no one can guarantee their occurrence. So how does an ordinary investor maximize gains in the market? What elements influence trends?

In this chapter we look into the factors that influence financial markets in order to help investors like you make sound decisions.

What drives stock price fluctuation?

In a typical farmer's market, prices are greatly influenced by supply and demand. Fruits during the in-season cost lower due to the abundance of supply. Hence, vendors in adjacent stalls compete to offer the most reasonable price to customers passing by. At the end of the day, they have to sell all the available stock before it spoils. On the other hand, fruits that are not in season cost higher due to limited supply. The customer who is willing to pay the highest or the best price (relative to the seller) wins, so to speak, the fruits.

The stock market operates in a similar manner. When more people want to buy a particular stock, the prices go up. Conversely, when people want to sell a particular stock, the prices go down. This is the natural order that can be observed in an environment governed by the law of supply and demand. Simple, right?

What complicates things is the presence of factors that influence the way people like or dislike a particular stock. It boils down to figuring out the positives and negatives of a particular company. Leaf through the business section, listen to the news and pay attention to the popular trends. This is one way to see what companies are hot.

What we will know is that people's sentiments play a significant role in driving price fluctuations. Perception and a company's reputation are two of the variables that can directly impact a stock price.

Perhaps Publicity?

Usually, bad publicity pulls down the prices. The main reason is that people see this information as a threat to the stability of the company and aims to get out quickly before their investments erode. Conversely, good publicity pulls up prices. Everybody wants to take part in the foreseen growth of a company and hence is willing to pay whatever price to own a share.

Perhaps Perception?

With this scenario, it can be observed that price movement is primarily influenced by how people perceive the worth of company. It has nothing to with the company's value.

The stock price does not reflect the actual value of a company in most cases.

Market Capitalization

Market capitalization gives you an idea about the value of a company. It is equivalent to the number of outstanding shares multiplied by the stock price. Consider this example, company ABC has two million outstanding shares having a stock price of $100/share, while company DEF has 10 million outstanding shares with a stock price of $50/share. Which of the two companies have a higher value? To evaluate these two companies, multiply the number of outstanding shares to the price:

Value of ABC = $100 x 2 million = $200 million

Value of DEF = $50 x 10 million = $500 million

Company DEF has a higher overall value compared to ABC since it had more outstanding shares. At first glance, ABC seems to have a higher value due to its higher price per share. When you want to compare the value of two companies, consider the market capitalization, not just the stock price.

Company Earnings

A company's earnings is an extremely important factor that can influence the value of the company as well at its stock price. It is equivalent to the total revenue minus the costs. Not a single business thrives without profits. What's the point of keeping it if you don't make any money?

In general, companies that generate increased earnings year after year usually have increasing stock prices. So how do they keep an uptrend in their profits? The following list shows some of the strategies applied by companies to achieve this goal:

  ☐ *Innovate*: There's always room improvement, as the cliché goes. Companies that continue to innovate are able to offer better products that make life more convenient for customers.

  A simple example is the invention of a ballpoint pen. With this product, the process of dipping a quill into an ink bottle is eliminated. Using this product also minimizes the risk of spilling ink all over your work. It is portable, convenient and the best part is that no animals are harmed in the process of production.

☐ *Exploring new markets*: With globalization, U.S. based brands have been exploring opportunities in foreign countries.

The model for this strategy is simple: tried and tested products or services are easier to sell to new markets. This is particularly effective for brands that have established their niche in their respective industries.

☐ *Establishing a brand name*: In blind taste tests, popular beverages rate comparably to generic beverages which are relatively much cheaper.

There's something in a name and packaging that makes some people willingly fork over more. Of course good advertising and other promotions help propel the popularity of a product. This must be coupled with staying true to what the brand promises

☐   *Managing costs*: Smart companies always control costs. It is a way to deliver your products and services at reasonable prices and more importantly, maximizes the profits. In some cases though, product quality is sacrificed and backfires in the form of dissatisfied customers.

Publicly listed companies are required to report their earnings quarterly. The Wall Street is particularly keen during these times since analysts calculate the future value of a company based on the earnings.

The stock price usually increases if a company earns more than expected. Otherwise, prices usually drop when a company performs worse than expected.

Chapter 7: Business Cycles and the Stock Market

Out of the thousands of government agencies collecting data on the economy, not one is concerned with dating business cycles. In America, this task falls to a private research organization, the National Bureau of Economic Research (NBER), founded in 1920. Its main purpose is to document business cycles and develop a series of national income accounts.

Wesley C. Mitchell, one of the founding members of the organization, together with Arthur Burns, renowned business cycle expert who later became the head of the Federal Reserve Board, define the business cycle. According to them, these cycles are considered a type of fluctuation primarily influenced by the economic activities of business enterprises.

The Business Cycle consists of three phases:

The first phase is the expansion phase described by lively and numerous activity and economic growth.

This is followed by the recession or contraction phase; economic activity slows down.

After which, the revival phase ensues. Economic activity begins to grow until the cycle renews.

This sequence of events recurs but is not periodic. The duration of one business cycle may vary from one company to another and may span from a year to about ten or more years.

The Business Cycle Committee of NREB confirms that from 1802 to 2006, the US has experienced 46 recessions. Each lasted for an average of 19 months, more than 50% lower than the average duration of expansions at 34 months.

This simply means that over the last 205 years, the economy has been in recession for about less than a third of the time. Dating a business cycle is important due to its social, political and economic implications. But how does it impact the stock market?

It has been observed that the stock market tends to rise ahead of recoveries and decline prior to recessions. Out of the 46 recessions since 1802, 42 have been preceded by declines in the stock return index. This is illustrated in the following

Recession	Peak of Stock Index (1)	Peak of Business Cycle (2)	Lead Time Between Peaks (3)	Decline in Stock Index from (1) to (2) (4)	Maximum 12 Month Decline in Stock Index (6)
1948-1949	May 1948	Nov 1948	6	-8.91%	-9.76%
1953-1954	Dec 1952	Jul 1953	7	-4.26%	-9.04%
1957-1958	Jul 1957	Aug 1957	1	-4.86%	-15.32%
1960-1961	Dec 1959	Apr 1960	4	-8.65%	-8.65%
1970	Nov 1968	Dec 1969	13	-12.08%	-29.16%
1973-1975	Dec 1972	Nov 1973	11	-16.29%	-38.80%
1980	Jan 1980	Jan 1980	0	0.00%	-9.55%
1981-1982	Nov 1980	Jul 1981	8	-4.08%	-13.99%
1990-1991	Jul 1990	Jul 1990	0	0.00%	-13.84%
2001	Aug 2000	Mar 2001	7	-22.94%	-26.55%
		Average	5.7	-8.21%	-17.47%

figure:

FIGURE 2. STOCK RETURNS DURING RECESSIONS

From this table you can see that the stock market seems to indicate an impending recession. The 1980 and 1990 recessions are exceptions of this case.   Yet, it can also trigger false alarms. Since 1802, there have been 12 instances wherein the returns index for stocks fell but was not followed by a recession within a year. Dating business cycles might seem irrelevant since the stock market do not actually reflect the status of businesses. However...

Can a business cycle then be used to gain in stocks? The answer is yes.

Investors who can time their strategies based on the peaks and troughs of economic activities can still gain significant returns. This is done by switching between fixed income instruments - such as bonds - and volatile investments - such as stocks - depending on the economic condition.

The returns from using this strategy are impressive.

By being able to predict the business cycle trough or peak a month before its occurrence leads to an annual increase of returns at a rate of 1.8% per year. This translates to a 60% increase in your wealth compared to the buy-and-hold strategy. The key here is to be skilled at identifying the stages of the business cycles. It also entails a lot of time to monitor your investments as well the current condition of the market.

PART III: Some Important Terms

Chapter 8: The Game Plan

The stock market may seem to be an exclusive world for financially savvy people.

It looks intriguing and mysterious enough to let people form various speculations ranging from logical observations (higher earnings are entail to higher risks) to the absurd ones (stock market is another form of gambling). Looking at graphs of prices and going through several jargons can be overwhelming for a beginning investor.

In learning a new field, it is always best to start with the basics.

The most common starting point is to get a grip on the most frequently used terms. Being able to comprehend and use these words will definitely help you appreciate how this system works, enable you to ask the right questions and allow you to decipher the investing strategies widely discussed by the industry experts. In the world of investing, it literally pays to know the basics.

In the previous part, we have discussed what stocks and stock markets are including the specific factors that influence stock prices. These next few chapters   delve into the other terms that you may encounter as you go on and learn about equity investing.

Chapter 9: Reading Stock Quotes

Stock quotes are popular symbolisms used in the business world.

The Wall Street Journal and Investor's Business Daily publish stock prices of the previous day. In cable channels such as Fox Business, Bloomberg and CNBC, you might have been distracted by the continuous stream of stock quotes as the program goes on.

The following table shows the types of information that you can obtain from looking at stock quotes online, while watching the news, and in the papers. In this example, the company is McDonald's Corporation with a trading symbol MCD. This is a sample code that can be used when checking stock prices of this particular company.

McDonald's Corporation (NYSE: MCD)

52-wk range	92.22 – 103.7

Last trade	March 25, 2014 6:42pm EDT
Change	-0.27 (-0.28%)
Day's range	95.83 – 96.49
Open	96.44
Volume	4,930,000
P/E ratio	17.27
Mkt cap	94.94B
Div/Yield	0.81/3.38

The following list describes the different entries found on the given table:

    ☐   **52 wk range**: This shows the price range of the MCD stock in the past 52 weeks; 92.22 is the lowest price attained while 103.7 is the highest price reached

52-wk range	92.22 – 103.7

☐   **Last trade**: This indicates the   last price at which the stock traded as well when it occurred; the information shows that this happened at 6:42pm eastern daylight time

Last trade   March   25, 2014 6:42pm EDT

☐   **Change**: This value indicates how much the current price differs from the previous day's closing price. In this example, the stock was down by 0.27 points equivalent to a decrease of 0.28% from the prior day's closing price.

Change   -0.27 (-0.28%)

☐   **Day's range**: These numbers indicate the lowest and highest prices at which the stock traded within the day

Day's range   95.83 – 96.49

☐   **Open**: This information tells you the stock price at the opening of the market

Open   96.44

☐   **Volume**: This figure indicates the number of shares that are traded currently. When the market closes, the volume indicates the total number of shares traded within one trading day.

Volume   4,930,000

☐   **P/E ratio**: It is a measure of the stock price with respect to the company's earnings. This entry is a benchmark used by investors an idea to gauge how cheaply, fairly or expensively a stock is valued.

P/E ratio   17.27

☐   **Market capitalization (Mkt cap)**: This number gives you the total market value of a company. As discussed in a previous chapter, it is calculated by multiplying the stock price with the total number of outstanding shares. In this example, the total market value of McDonald's is 4.93Million US dollars.

Mkt cap   94.94B

☐ **Latest Dividend/ Dividend yield**: The latest dividend figure shows the amount per share paid to each stockholder during the most recent quarter. The dividend yield is equivalent to the value of the latest dividend multiplied to the number of times the dividends are paid each year then divided by the stock price. This number indicates how much yield the stock's dividend produces.

Div/Yield   0.81/3.38

And there you have it. Now that have been equipped with these basic definitions, looking into stock quotes should not be such an overwhelming task.

Using the P/E ratio, you can now evaluate and compare stocks within the same industry.

If you want to know which stocks are actively traded in the market, you can check out the volume of traded stocks for that particular moment.

Itching to know the market value of a particular company? Look into its market capital.

Stock quotes provide a summary of the overall financial status of a company. Being able to interpret this information can serve as a powerful guide in assessing the viability of a stock.

Chapter 10: What type of Investor are you?

After establishing your emergency fund and following your set budget, you now have some money to spare for investments.

Before jumping into investing you might want to consider and ask yourself some simple questions:

Are you a risk taker?

Or are you risk averse?

Are you willing to throw money for a chance to make more? Or are you content in a small but regular income? Can you sleep at night knowing that you just incurred 50% of potential loss? Your answers to these questions will tell you a lot about your investing appetite.

Bulls and bears are not exclusive to farms (and the NBA...). The stock market has a fair share of these creatures too. This chapter discusses some of the types of players in this arena. Read on to find out what type of investor are you.

Market types:

☐ **Bulls**: A bull market is a favorable environment where everything in the economy is doing well; people can easily find jobs, businesses are expanding, the gross domestic product is growing and stock prices continue to soar. In this context, a person is considered a bull if he or she is optimistic and firmly believes that the stock prices will go up. But just like any phase, the bull market does not last forever. Markets follow cycles right?

☐ **Bears**: Contrary to the bull market, a bear market is characterized by a bad economy. Businesses downsize making it difficult for people to find jobs. A recession is expected to occur within the next period which why stock prices decline. In this case, a person is considered a bear if he or she believes that stock prices will eventually drop. Bear markets are tough times to spot profitable stocks.

One strategy to survive this market is to hold shares until the bear market ends.

Investor Types:

☐ **Chickens**: Risk averse investors are collectively referred to as chickens. They fear losing money and hence tend to invest in fixed income instruments or tend to get out of markets as quickly as possible. The downside is that investments are not given ample time to grow and, hence, their returns are minimal if not none at all.

☐ **Pigs**: Extreme risk takers are referred to as pigs. Their aim is get high returns at the quickest possible time. They invest in hot tips and get in and out of markets without doing proper research. They usually get leads from fellow pigs. Their goal is to earn money regardless if they have little knowledge of the ins and outs of an investment scheme. They are impatient, emotionally attached to their investments and are most vulnerable to losses.

Investing strategies abound. One person may find a particular investing style effective while another person may not agree. Bulls and bears may constantly be at odds. But the important thing is that they hopefully understand the dynamics of the market in order to apply the style that they are most comfortable with. At the end of the day we all want to make some money. Knowing yourself and what you're getting into will save you from incurring a negative portfolio.

PART IV: Let's Start Investing!

If you have reached this point, Congratulations! The previous sections have introduced you to some terms used by traders as well as some basic concepts on how stock markets work. In this section we look at ways on how to get into the market. Useful tips for successful stock investing have also been included in this section.

http://virtual-stock-exchange.com/

PRACTICE: Your Stock Investing Demo Account

If you have reached this point, Congratulations! The previous sections have introduced you to some terms used by traders as well as some basic concepts on how stock markets work.

In the next few chapters, we look at ways on how to get into the market. Useful tips for successful stock investing have also been included.

To enhance your skills, familiarize and test yourself with virtual stock exchanges. Here are some to start:

http://www.marketwatch.com/game/stock-market-simulator

http://capitaloption.com/lp/en/beginners3/?coc=1&subc=35326_2499092

http://uk.saxomarkets.com/online-trading/stock-trading

Chapter 11: Methods of Buying Stocks

Now that you know what stocks are, and have a bit of knowledge on the stock market principles, you feel more confident to be part of the exchange. So how do you go about it? What instruments are available to people who want to trade?

Once you decide to invest in stocks, a lot of options exist to get you started. You can either invest in a managed fund or create your own portfolio with the help of your stock broker.

Buying stocks through mutual funds

A mutual fund is a type of investment vehicle wherein money is taken from different investors and pooled into a single fund. This money is invested in a mix of securities and fixed-income assets in order to make it grow.

Mutual funds are professionally managed funds. It is the fund manager who calls the shots as to where to invest the money - as well as the percentages allocated for each type of security. Stock mutual funds invest primarily in stocks.

If you're too busy to monitor your trades, or are in doubt of your investing instincts, then this can be the best investment for you.

Stock mutual funds have diversified portfolios because the fund manager ensures that maximum profits are reaped most of the time. In essence availing mutual funds has two advantages: Diversification and professional management.

If you like to be in control, mutual funds might not be your cup of tea. By joining a fund, you are giving the fund manager the power to control the allocation of the group's assets as he or she deems suitable. Some people are uncomfortable with this idea because you don't physically have a say in what they do to the fund.

Another drawback of mutual funds is tax concerns. Some funds may produce high levels of taxable distributions. The solution to this is to choose tax-friendly funds.

Availing exchange traded funds

Exchange-traded funds (ETFs) are shares issued by an investment company designed to track an underlying portfolio, such as indices.

ETFs work like mutual funds - except that these are traded in the stock market. Its selling point is the lower operating expenses compared to mutual funds. Another advantage over mutual funds is that an investor can sell ETFs short. Doing so goes with the hope that the shares can be bought back at a lower price. This strategy is applied by investors who want to lock in profits in case the market drops.

In the 1990s, most of the ETFs tracked only the well-known indices such as S & P 500 and the Dow. Currently customized indices are also being tracked and managed by investment companies.

Hedge Funds

A Hedge fund is basically an investment partnership. The parties involved are the fund manager, which can be considered the general partner, and the investors, who can also be called limited partners.

The purpose of a hedge fund is to maximize returns while eliminating risks. Unlike mutual funds, this type of investment is only open to investors who have a certain net worth, say for example, $1 million.

Another feature of hedge funds is that it can be used to invest in just about anything, from currencies to securities and even real estate.

One disadvantage is the steep management fees. Hedge funds charge an asset management fee (1.0 to 2%) and a performance fee (equivalent to 20% cut from the gains).

At first glance, hedge funds seem to be enticing investments. Imagine being able to reap gains in the face of a bear market. Yet to eliminate further risks, investors both new and experienced should still take time to study and understand this investment vehicle.

Choosing stocks on your own

Building your own portfolio can both be a challenging and exciting experience. It supports the idea that you should take responsibility for your own finances. It doesn't necessarily imply though that you should do literally everything on your own. For one, you can rely on company reports when you do your research on a particular stock. Also, you can avail the services of a broker in order to make trades.

Compared to the other methods previously discussed, this step entails a lot of studying and analysis on the part of the investor - yet it give the best learning experience.

The goal is to become adept at spotting stocks that are reasonably priced and can give good returns. Professional investors devote about 80 hours each week for investing. Not a lot of people can spend this much time just for studying stocks and the markets. In any case, it is important to make some time to at least understand how the system works.

As in any type of investments, there are no guarantees to returns. The constants are risks and the possibility to lose. Each stock investing method has its own set of risks. By carefully studying each method, an investor can properly assess the most suitable instrument that can help realize his/her goals.

IMPORTANT NOTE:

Be wary of any group-type investment deals that offer "X% return guaranteed" or anything of that nature. By law, it's illegal for the Financial Services industry to promote investment vehicles with lines like "returns guaranteed". Because, by nature, no returns are 100% guaranteed; there will be losses at times. If someone tries to promote that to you, it might be a ponzi scheme or something similarly dangerous.

Chapter 12: Important tips for successful Investing

Be careful with short-term trade or attempting to time the market

What is the best time to invest? Well, anytime is the best time to invest. You cannot predict how the market will behave since it is influenced by more than a dozen factors including human sentiment. Stocks are profitable long term investments. Its inherent volatility makes it unattractive as short term investments.

Unfortunately, some investors who closely monitor their investments are often tempted to sell their stocks after short holding periods. This is often triggered by reactions to stock price increase or decrease. As a result, they either get minimal gains or none at all. The worst case is that when these minimum gains are eaten up by taxes and other fund fees.

Use Cost Averaging

One strategy that can be used is cost averaging. This method involves buying a fixed number of shares (worth $100 for example) of a blue chip company at regular intervals, say once a month or quarterly.

With this technique, you can buy more shares at the same price when the market is down and just enough shares when the market is high. In the end, your average cost is still lower than the highest price reached by a stock. Hence, you can still gain profits.

Diversify

You've probably heard this before: Don't put all your eggs in one basket. In part 1, we have discussed how different-sized companies vary in terms of performance. While there is no solid guideline as to how portfolios must be allocated, several resources can give you a hint on how to distribute your funds. If you're hesitant to start from scratch, you can always follow the portfolio of popular indices. In applying this strategy, you can first study how this portfolio performs, then you can later decide on which stocks to retain and which to include. It helps to evaluate your total returns and expenses at least once a year. This will give you an overview of your investment's performance.

About Penny Stocks

A word of caution: be careful of penny stocks. These are stocks of small companies that have low prices per share ranging from pennies to a few dollars hence its name. Although not all of these companies have a bleak prospect, most of them do. Which is why buying a lot in bulk might prove to be a big mistake in the long run. Initially, a hype is created by penny-stock brokers to encourage people to buy. As interest increases, the stock price goes up and up, until it reaches its peak. At this point, people eventually discover that there's not much in that company's prospects that is worth investing. Prices go down and you're eventually left with losses.

On the other hand, there IS gain in this strategy somehow. However, if you want to go this route, tread carefully.

Minimize trading costs

Trading costs in the form of management fees, taxes and commissions may be eating up a significant portion of your returns. If you are investing through a broker or a financial advisor, you might want to consider the corresponding fees charged to you for their services.

Also, you might want to rethink if you really need an advisor:

Are you getting unbiased help?

Is his/her advice financially sound?

As you learn your way around the market, you might just have to consult an expert from time to time or turn to other references to validate your assumptions.

Watch for Broker Honesty

Be on a lookout for broker conflicts of interest. If you invest in individual stock through brokers that earn from commissions, you might want to reconsider their research wherein they tell you which stocks to buy, hold, or sell. Brokerage analysts who, with best intentions, write negative reviews of a company find their careers stalled in a several ways.

For instance, companies that are criticized tend to exclude the critiquing analyst from meetings regarding the company. Hence, those analysts who want to keep their jobs avoid writing negative reports. (Although there are still those who do their best to give honest reviews.)

Be keen on taxes

Taxes are considered an additional trading expense. You can minimize this cost by investing in tax-advantages accounts. The best defense is your knowledge of what and how items are taxed and by how much. So read as much as possible on this matter. To have an idea on how taxes affect your returns, always calculate annual returns with an after-tax basis.

Avoid overconfidence

Good for you if you have decided to pick your own stocks. However don't be easily swayed by do-it-yourself guides that claim that you can beat and even exceed the market returns.

As a newbie investor, you definitely have to dedicate a portion of your time to read financial statements and company reports. Picking stocks is not an easy job. Fund managers, who have spent almost their entire life in this field, can attest to that. Do your homework. Know what you're getting into.

PRACTICE: Your Move, the Next Steps

Now it's time.

If you are ready to invest or trade in the real world, take your pic at any of the following top online stock exchanges below:

QuestTrade: www.questrade.com

TD Ameritrade: www.tdameritrade.com

OptionsHouse: www.optionshouse.com

E*Trade: us.etrade.com

Re-read and refresh yourself with the material in the book, until the stock market feels natural to you.

And even then, be disciplined. If your goal is financial freedom through stock investing, follow the course until you're successful.

IMPORTANT NOTES:

If it's one thing about making money through investment vehicles, it's this.

The higher the risk, the higher the reward. So, if you want to gain more, you better have the guts to be willing to lose more.

So, if you want to make money within your first few hours, be well-educated. Read well, research well, and take the plunge. Rejoice if you gain, brace yourself and carry on if you lose.

And remember: if there's any investment offers out there with tag lines like "GUARANTEED RETURN ON INVESTMENT", back away. The FTC states this as illegal. By nature, almost every investment vehicle out there is somewhat volatile: while some investments gain a lot, some investments lose a lot too.

PART V: Deep, Insightful Stock Market Research

Chapter 13: How to Research

The most challenging part of making money on the stock market is researching the companies you want to invest in. If you've decided to become an active investor instead of using mutual funds or ETF's (Exchange Traded Funds), where you're passive, you have to find a way to pick the best stocks to invest in. Where do you find the information that you need, and what is it, exactly, that you should be looking for?

One way to go about it is to use an Investment Research company such as Morningstar. Services like these will be able to gather all the pertinent information for you into one place, and save you loads of time, for a fee. On the other hand, you'll be making decisions based on the recommendation of someone else, and in the end, you'll want to know for yourself. Fortunately most of this information is available to you, if you're prepared to look. Also, there are lots of free tools available on the internet to point you in a good direction, and get you started out. Some of these include:

Investopedia – This is a great place for the beginner. You can pick up stock picking tips, and look up information about stocks.

The Wall Street Journal – They've been around for decades in print form, and now that they are online, it is so much easier to find articles on just about any investment you're thinking of.

Also try: Yahoo! Finance, MSN Money, Investor Guide and Seeking Alpha.

These are all good sources of the information you need to get you going. Once you've identified, generally, the type of stocks you're aiming at, you'll want to go deeper into the specifics.

Chapter 14: Going Deeper

A Stock Screener is a tool that you need to master. This is something that you can use to filter, or screen investment opportunities (stocks or companies) by different sets of criteria, all customizable and user-defined. There are a number of Stock Screeners to choose from online, so spend some time choosing the best one for you. Here are a few free ones to look at:

Finviz.com

ChartMill.com

Zacks.com

Trade-Ideas.com

Find one that makes sense to you, and that you're comfortable using. This will narrow your search into the vast number of stocks on offer to a limited number of options that you can then decide to pick apart in detail. At this point you'll need to find more information about the specific candidates you've selected.

A good place to start is to find the SEC (Securities and Exchange Commission) Filings for the company you want to research. By law, companies have to report financials periodically on Forms 10-k and 10-Q. These reports are organized by EDGAR (Electronic Data Gathering, Analysis and Retrieval system), and can be found at: http://www.sec.gov. The database can easily be searched by Ticker Symbol, State or Country, or even by industry. The 10-K form is the primary source for audited financial statements, and most of the important facts about the company, but the listings contain a whole range of information.

Trade magazines offer a good place to do more digging. You can find out about the particular industry or sector that you mean to invest in, see what the current trends are, what difficulties companies face, and who the market leaders are. Compare this to the business plan and marketing strategy of the company you have your eye on.

Company News is another great place to look. Use a search engine to see what the company is saying about itself, and what customers and competitors say about the same subject. Take everything "with a pinch of salt" and make up your own mind. Remember, the numbers and charts, though vital, are only one side of the story. Try to find out how people, especially the customers and employees, feel about the company.

You can't know everything, so decide for yourself what is most important to know, and concentrate the search until you find the core data. It is more than likely that you will be able to find far more information about any particular company or industry than you will be able to digest in a limited amount of time, so you need a system to make your hard work efficient and goal driven. This way you'll have better success in a shorter time.

Create a Scoring System

Create a system for yourself to score the companies you research based on what you believe are the vital elements for your decision. Profitability, market share, and Earnings per share should be on the list, but add whatever else you believe is key, and simply drop what you believe is not vital. Keep the list short – between 5 and 15 areas of criteria should be sufficient, and you can always fine tune the system as you go along. Then focus on only those areas, scoring in an uncomplicated way – a simple "pass" or "fail" could work, or alternatively score 1 for bad, 2 for mediocre and 3 for good.

Example: For Profitability, or Revenue, score "pass" or 3 if the company is increasing the amount of money coming in, score 2 for a stable revenue, and score either "fail" or 1 for a decreasing revenue. Then tally up the scores and compare the companies this way.

BONUS: Avoiding Investment Scams

Along with the fine benefits that the internet offers, allowing us unprecedented ease of research, investigation and number-crunching, there is the inevitable threat of fraud and dishonesty. We all know about email scams, mobile phone scams and the like. There are unscrupulous people out there who will appeal to your greed, and gullibility. We often see news headlines about one or other filthy rich person who has cheated investors, and spent huge sums of money on his own lavish lifestyle. If you're going to be dealing with large sums of money online, you need to be aware of some of the ways that professional scam artists use to separate you from your hard earned gains.

Here are some of the most common scams to watch out for:

Ponzi Schemes: This is where funds from one investor are used to provide payment to previous investors. Like a Pyramid scheme, when the funds owed to an investor are greater than the available funds, the scheme collapses, and you're left with nothing. The scheme always collapses.

Pump and Dump: Sometimes a group of people who are "in-the know" will collaborate to invest in particular stocks, then create hype, recommending these stocks to thousands of other investors. What happens is that the increased demand pushes stock prices up very quickly, at which point they will all sell off their stocks at huge profit, and the victims are left with the ensuing losses. This often happens with OTC (Over the counter) stocks, for which information is less readily available. Watch out for anyone pressuring you to buy into a particular stock, promising unrealistic profits, and offering vague information about the deal. Once again, it pays to do your homework!

Affinity Fraud: The scam artist approaches well known or respected individuals in groups, such as churches or societies, and uses this leverage to gain more and more members for his "investment" scheme. Once he has gathered enough money, and before the promised return on investment is due, he simply disappears with everyone's money. Often the individual will use authentic looking web sites and documentation to convince his victims.

Bulletin Boards and Social Media: Social media, blogs and bulletin boards are full of all kinds of information. Much of it is useful, and you can learn a thing or two about an industry or trends in the thinking related to many different areas. The trouble with most of these is that users remain anonymous, and fraudsters capitalize on this to shamelessly promote their illegal enterprises. It is virtually impossible to sift out the real thing from the fake, and you're likely to invest your money into something you will regret.

In conclusion, watch out for someone who tries to pressure you into an "unbelievable opportunity" which is available to only a select group. More than likely, he is trying to use your own greed against you. If the facts about the deal seem vague, or hidden, if it is offered to you "on the side" without verifiable, legitimate documentation, it is better to think twice. If the seller tries to create a sense of urgency for you to invest before the opportunity is lost – beware. The old cliché remains true – if it sounds too good to be true, more than likely it isn't.

PART VI: The World's Greatest Stock Investors, and their Investing Methods

Chapter 15: Learn from the Best

Going into the stock market with good intentions, but no plan, is bound to lead to disaster. It would be better to try your luck at the Roulette tables. On the other hand, there is no hard and fast rule to becoming successful. Investors who have made considerable gains will often disagree about the best strategy. However, most would agree that you need a plan. So let's take one or two of the most famous and wealthy investors of all time, and have a look at what their approach was. You can take from their success stories what you believe is wise, and significantly improve your own strategy.

Warren Buffet

"Look at market fluctuations as your friend rather than your enemy; profit from folly rather than participate in it."

Born August 30th, 1930, Warren Buffet is widely considered one of the greatest investors of modern times. Known as the

"Wizard of Omaha" or the "Sage/Oracle of Omaha", he has consistently ranked amongst the world's wealthiest, and exerts considerable influence in the world of international finance, even advising Presidents on occasion. He is also a philanthropist, promising to donate his vast wealth to charity when he and his wife leave this earth, and has publically spoken out against what he perceives to be social injustices caused by the current economic system. What can we learn from this man?

First of all, Buffet keeps his strategies simple, and thinks long-term, instead of turning quick profits. He maintains that it is more important to invest in high quality companies at a fair price than to invest in low quality companies at a low price. In the end, you get what you pay for.

Rather than thinking of stocks as faceless entities, Buffet believes in investing in what he knows, and tries to improve the companies he invests him by improving management and resourcefulness. He similarly uses a scoring system, based on 12 tenets, or key points about the company to consider. He focuses on the management of a company, asking whether or not the management is rational, and whether they are honest with shareholders. These are difficult questions to answer, but he believes they are key to his long-term success.

 He reportedly focuses on Return on Equity (ROE) rather than earnings per share, which is contrary to many accepted theories of investing, based on the idea that ROE can be influenced by leverage. Buffet prefers to look at leverage separately, showing once again that no single approach is always the winning answer.

Benjamin Graham

"Though business conditions may change, corporations and securities may change, and financial institutions and regulations may change, human nature remains the same. Thus the important and difficult part of sound investment, which hinges upon the investor's own temperament and attitude, is not much affected by the passing years."

Benjamin Graham (Grossbaum) 1894-1976 is considered the father of value investing, which means buying stocks that are priced lower than their intrinsic value, or book value, using a form of security analysis. He was the mentor of , among others, Warren Buffet, discussed above, as well as Charlie Munger, Irving Kahn and Walter J Schloss who all went on to become hugely successful in their own rights. He was an inspirational teacher, and highly influential in world economy. He devised a new basis for both US and global currency.

Graham was hesitant to take risks. His approach was conservative. He was not swayed by flash in the pan gains and losses, but concentrated instead on a company's balance sheets, and its fundamentals, their amount of debt, their sales figures. His fundamental strategy was the "margin of safety" – a measure of the stock's trading price as related to the value of the company itself. The higher the margin of safety; the better the investment.

Seth Klarman

"You cannot ignore the market – ignoring a source of investment opportunities would obviously be a mistake – but you must think for yourself and not allow the market to direct you."

Born 1957, Seth Klarman is an American Billionaire who founded the Baupost Group. He wrote the book: *Margin of Safety, Risk averse Investing for the Thoughtful Investor*, which is now out of print, but second-hand copies reach between $1500 and $2000. He is hesitant to give away more of his secrets about the best investment strategies.

Klarman entered the market a little later than the previous two examples, and facing a more crowded marketplace, his strategy differs a little from theirs. He believes that going against the grain, doing things that others don't can give him the necessary advantage. Thousands of people are competing for the same "deal", but sometimes the trick is to buy stocks that others do not see the value of. He finds opportunities in smaller 'spin-offs' of larger companies, and regularly researches bankrupt companies, or companies in distress. If these are able to make a comeback, the gains can be sizeable.

Klarman focuses on risk factors, often looking into foreign investment opportunities where the socio-political environments pose different challenges. He also believes in looking at the company behind the numbers, rather than making a decision based on computer analysis alone. He cautions new investors to focus on cash flow rather than profits, and to evaluate balance sheets for risks like too much debt or big pension fund liabilities. He further reasons that it is safer to rely on bond coupons or stock dividends for your income than relying on the fickle market for capital gains.

Timothy Sykes

Born as recently as 1981, Tim Sykes is an exception to the rule. A newcomer to the world of Investing, this young man became famous by investing money which he received for his bar mitzvah while still in high school. He began day trading in penny stocks. Before the age of 21 he had turned this into $1.65 million. This goes to prove, once again, that anything can happen on the stock market.

Between 2006 and 2007 Sykes turned to investing, rather than trading, and suffered considerable losses. He took this as a challenge, and started again with a sum identical to his original bar-mitvah money, and once again made considerable gains.

In an interview with Forbes.com, Sykes reveals a little part of his strategy for dealing with the market. He says: "My risk tolerance is simple: if a stock doesn't act EXACTLY the way I thought it would when I first entered the trade, I get out. It doesn't matter if I have a small profit or small loss, low priced stocks move so quickly-and I'm trading the most volatile of the bunch-that I can't risk getting stuck in a pattern I'm not 100% sure about." (Forbes.com)

From these masters of the trade we can learn valuable lessons that we can study, emulate, and adjust to suit our needs. The most important lessons are to gain a deep understanding of the companies, people and organizations we are investing in. Stocks are more than just numbers on a screen, or points in a graph. Behind the statistics are people, with hopes, wishes and dreams of their own. Our goal is to generate income, and the path that we choose can make it either full of risk and uncertainty, or full of reward. There is always more to learn, and there is always a hidden problem. The better your research, and the more effective your strategy, the fewer "unknowns" will pop up and ruin your chances. Make sure you've done your homework, weigh up the options carefully, and at the end of the day you can be assured of achieving the goal you set yourself.

Conclusion

Thank you again for downloading this book!

I hope this book was able to help you.

The next step is to apply what you've learned.

Finally, if you enjoyed this book, please take the time to share your thoughts and post a review on Amazon. It'd be greatly appreciated!

If you truly received value from this book, then I'd like to ask you a favor.

Would you be kind and courteous enough to leave a good review on Amazon?

I aim to reach as many like-minded people as I can with this book. More reviews will help me accomplish that! Also, if you happen to be a writer or any type of artist as well, you may even have some good karma; your odds of having more great reviews for your books increases :)

P.S. Things change. Trends change. And so will this book. As a token of appreciation for your commitment to downloading this book, enjoy all the free updates to this book version in the future. Take care.

BONUS: Successful Real Estate Investing

Courtesy of FR Commerce, enjoy a few free chapters of our other books.

If you want to learn more, please visit the Book Page.

"Makin' Money with Real Estate"

Increase in property value

The value of properties does not always increase and this can be seen during the past few years. These values cannot even beat inflation. For instance you purchased a piece of property worth $500,000 and. You may be able to sell the property for $515,000 after a year when the inflation rate is at 3% but you will notice that that $15,000 profit does not affect your purchasing power since its value is the same as when you purchased it. How is that so? The profit you received was not real it was merely enough to cover the inflation rate during that year hence you are not actually

$15,000 richer than you were the year before. This kind of situation arises when the government has to make money but it spends more than it has collected in taxes.

You must be asking how then do investors make money with their real estate holdings? These investors make money when they take advantage of a situation where in the rate of inflations is predicted to exceed the current rate of long-term debt. You will notice that there are people purchasing properties and they are even willing to take out a loan to purchase those properties. These people are willing to take the risk because they are paying off the mortgage of those purchased properties with dollars which are worth less than their value. This shows a saver becoming a debtor. In fact, a lot of investors made money this way in the 1970s and the early 1980s when the inflation was spiraling out of control.

Rental Income

Making money from renting out property is a very lucrative source of income. A great illustration of that would be a game of monopoly. If one has interest in a house, an apartment building, a hotel or an office building then you can rent those out and collect rent in exchange for letting them utilize those buildings.

A useful tool in making money from these properties is the capitalization rate. This rate is a special financial ratio in which the value for which the property can be sold is divided by the value in which they earn per year. For instance, your apartment building may be sold for a million dollars and it earns one hundred thousand dollars a year. One million dollars is divided by the hundred thousand dollars which gives us a ratio of 10 percent. Thus, you can expect a 10 percent return on your investment if you purchased said property in cash and without any debt in acquiring it.

Business Operations

This type of operation involves business activities and special services. For instance, you are the owner of an office building and you may generate income through vending machines placed in the building and for pay parking. You are able to earn income not just by renting your property out but by providing income generating services that are incidental to you renting it out or to a business that you operate.

BONUS: Successful Options Trading

Courtesy of FR Commerce, enjoy a few free chapters of our other books.

If you want to learn more, please visit the Book Page.

" A lot of people are afraid to try options trading. They feel that it is so complex that only scientists can understand it.

But, there's no need to be so hesitant.

Because the basics of option trading are easy to understand - there's a good learning experience here that helps those who need the guidance.

First, you may not realize it, but you can essentially control the underlying assets - the stock, bond, or other commodity within the option contract - within the given time frame. You have the "option" (no pun intended) to buy, sell, hand over the rights, or just hold on to them. Did the stock price suddenly skyrocket? Imagine buying that same stock for a really low price. Did the stock price suddenly drop?

Imagine selling that same stock at the original price. Your choices are virtually endless.

Next, Some investors prefer buying options instead of the underlying asset because the former is cheaper to buy than the latter. Furthermore, they can control the number of shares for a lesser price.

The first two parts introduce you to the world of options. They differentiate between stocks themselves and the options bound to them. They also show you how options work and all the terms options use.

The next parts will send you into the fire: you will be armed with various strategies, as well as do's and don'ts as you start your options campaign.

If you feel more than confident enough to take on the real world of options, try your hand on the real money online exchanges - and trade your way into victory. "

Options and Leveraging, for example:

Let's say an investor purchased 100 shares of a particular company stock at $100 each. Therefore, it has cost him $10,000. However, he also has five $200 premium call options each with a $100/share strike price, which will allow him the right to purchase 500 shares as well.

If after 1 month the share price rose to $110, the gain on his stocks is $1,000. However, what if the option premium for the same stock also increases - to $300 for each whole contract?. For the regular stock investment, the gain is 10%; for his stock option values, the gain is 50%.

But for ALL the underlying stocks within his five options, he can exercise all the options, buying 500 more originally at $50,00 overall, then SELLING them back at $55,000 - that's a $5,000 profit.

Leveraging has its disadvantages, too. If the price didn't move to the right direction, the percentage lost is magnified.

Using the same example, if the share price fell to $80 ($10 lower than the option's strike price), the loss is 20%. On the other hand, the option premium might decrease to $80, or a 60% percentage loss overall.

As such, an investor must exercise caution in using leveraging when trading options.

Time Frame

A regular stock has no expiration date. It means that the stockholder can hold onto his stocks indefinitely. On the other hand, a stock option has an expiration date. An out-of-the-money option only becomes worthless when it is not exercised prior to its expiration date.

Ownership

Ownership of a share of stock is proven by a certificate issued by the company. A stock option doesn't have a certificate of ownership; whoever holds it owns it.

Volume

A company can only issue a fixed number of shares. Therefore, investors can only trade a limited number of shares.

On the other hand, there us no limit as to the number of stock options investors can buy or sell. A stock option doesn't offer dividends, voting rights, or ownership of the company if the option isn't exercised.

Market Exchanges

Professional traders, individual investors, and institutions trade options on an options exchange. It is possible for an entity to transact a lot of options contracts at the same time.

Like regular stocks, a stock option is traded on a market regulated by SEC. Brokers facilitate the options transactions just like the regular stocks. Monitoring of transactions and performances are easily done through their respective marketplaces.

BONUS: Successful Forex Trading

Courtesy of FR Commerce, enjoy a few free chapters of our other books.

If you want to learn more, please visit the Book Page.

"Introduction"

You know how that saying goes, "Money makes the world go round".

Nowadays, for you or anyone to live comfortably, you should have enough money to buy the things you need. Food, shelter, water, a way to get around, everything.

However, a lot of people are currently experiencing that gruelling feeling of living from paycheck to paycheck and they are barely surviving the day. Since their job would probably take most of their hours in a day, there is not much time for them to take on another job. And trust me, a lot of colleague, friends, and myself have been there. It sucks. Period.

There are several options that you can take in order to solve this problem: one is to scrimp on the daily necessities and save up (and invest in time deposits, mutual funds or stocks), and another is to find other ways to make money without hurting your day job. The first one is definitely painful; to do away with enjoying life and its luxuries just to save a meager amount isn't fair. What's the point of saving up if you don't make enough money in the first place? That leaves everyone to resort to the other, better option.

Through foreign exchange trading, you can definitely make money in the comfort of your home and at your own pace. With the advent of technology, trading through the foreign exchange, or forex for short, has become a lot easier; everyone can trade with other people from anywhere in the world.

Forex is definitely advantageous compared to other investment vehicles. In forex, you trade yours or people's money through an online platform to gain a profit. And there is no person in the world who doesn't need money, so there will always be somebody who is willing to buy forex. It's very easy to sell; that's why the profits are instantaneous – no more waiting time needed unlike in other investments such as time deposits and mutual funds.

More importantly, there is an unlimited earning potential in forex. In other financial instruments, such as savings deposit and fixed income securities, the income is already defined by the fund manager. In forex, it is you, the trader, who has the control of the earnings.

This book will teach you how to start trading successfully in forex and make your money work for you - literally.

"What is Foreign Exchange Trading?"

Foreign exchange is the biggest financial market in the world - with a global market value of $5 trillion.

Forex is simply the process of exchanging a currency with another currency on its current exchange rate.

The exchange is done primarily because of commerce and tourism. For example, let's say a person is travelling to Japan. He will exchange his US dollars for Japanese yen so he could pay for the things he needs when in Japan.

In the business sector, products and services may come from a different country. Let's say, a US car company may import parts from Japan and thus have to pay the products in Japanese yen. So again, the exchange is required, which is usually done by the companies' banks.

Because of the massive exchange of currencies every day, among many factors, it creates a difference in the value of the currencies being traded. This price difference creates a financial opportunity, which is now called forex market trading.

What is Forex Market Trading?

Banks who were originally trading currencies for their clients saw this opportunity and began trading their money - in the hopes that the currency they bought will increase in value. They also hope that the currency they sold will be weaker in the near in the near future.

Although the difference is small, if trading in enormous amounts, this small price difference in buying and selling currencies can still rake in millions in profits within a single day. Yes, it's possible, though it's usually a larger-scale operation.

This opportunity to trade currencies was then sought out and grabbed by large corporations, multinational companies, a few wealthy private individuals, and hedge funds.

Basically, forex market trading is the process of buying and selling currencies with the goal of making *profit from the price difference. It's just buy-low, sell-high, only with currency.*

Country	Currency	Symbol
United States	US dollar	USD
Euro Zone Members	Euro	EUR
Japan	Japanese yen	JPY
reat Britain	Pound	GBP
Switzerland	Swiss franc	CHF
Canada	Canadian dollar	CAD
Australia	Australian dollar	AUD
ew Zealand	New Zealand dollar	NZD

Major Currencies

Anyone in the world can participate in the forex market and trade their own currency against any other currency.

However, just like any industry, there will always be major participants.

Below is a short list of major currencies being traded and their corresponding symbols:

It is important to become familiar with the currency symbols as these symbols are used when trading.

The first two letters of the currency symbol is from the country's name and the last letter is from its currency's name.

For Switzerland, the symbol is CHF as Switzerland's official name, which is in Latin, is Confoederatio Helvetica. "

Copyright Notice